My Little ~~Book~~ of Helpfulness

GW00648232

The Endless Bookcase
71 Castle Road
St Albans
Hertfordshire
England UK
AL1 5DQ

www.theendlessbookcase.com

This booklet is available in a variety of formats both paper and electronic.

Check www.theendlessbookcase.com for availability.

ISBN: 978-1-908941-66-4

Acknowledgements

I would like to express my sincere thanks to Gail Hugman of Lessons Alive, if it wasn't for Gail this little book would never have come into existence. Nick Pelekanos of Pelekan Designs for his wonderful design. He was able to interpret my thoughts and vision for design when I couldn't put those thoughts into words. In other words he "got me". Carl French and Morgana Evans from The Endless Bookcase for their help and guidance. My sister Sharon for her support, but most of all, you, my readers.

Thank you all.

"Stress is Like a Violin String. Too much Tension and the String will Snap, Too Little and it will not Produce any Music. However, Just the Right Amount of Tension Produces Vibrant Energy"

Anon

Reviews

"This is brilliant! I love it. I immediately understand what to do, how to do it and what result I should get.

It's simple, straightforward, clear and people will clamour to have one in 'their back pocket'. Please do more. I need it. The world needs it."

Gail Hugman, Lessons Alive.

"Very, very good!!

"It depicted easily digestible and powerful tools to support us so affected by everyday issues.

"The book further cuts away a lot of meaningless words to help the reader stay tuned to working on achievable goals with significant outcomes. I enjoyed it and see it as not a novella but a book of significant tools that can be quickly grasped."

Anthony Rhone, Psychotherapist & Counsellor.

"Amazing!! In a world full of pressure and stress, help at last in a small book that everyone can understand and use. I am sure it will become the "little black book" that everyone wants to own."

Sue Arfin, Holistic Health Lab.

"A little book with BIG ideas, top tips and sound advice to get you back on track and back to the real you."

David Clarke, Rock PR.

"What a great little book. I only wish it had been around during my working life. Now I have retired to the countryside, a lot of stress has disappeared from my life, but even now I found some tips really useful, like how to stop procrastinating and get a job done! An easy to follow guide that could really make a difference to readers' lives."

Stephen Plosker, France.

"Monica has condensed a lifetime's experience of what really works into her book "My Little book of Helpfulness" which comprises of 17 "Helpfulness Techniques" that can be practiced, in a few minutes each day, to minimise a whole range of stressful situations. The techniques are very accessible and easy to learn. They can be used by anyone suffering from stress or the associated low self-esteem and lack of confidence. For this reason it could be very useful to any manager, looking to build confidence and a feeling of helpfulness in their teams at work. We all know that defensiveness destroys initiative. This "Little Book" can help your business."

Nick Brown - Author 'Thrive and Survive in Business'.

About the Author

Monica Black is Master Clinical Hypnotherapist, Master NLP Practitioner, an EMDR Practitioner, Coach, Mindfulness Teacher, Trainer and Media Commentator.

Monica began practicing in 2000, after leaving a stressful life in the city, thus making her exceptionally well qualified to help those dealing with the stresses and strains of modern day living,

Using her 'tool box' of Hypnotherapy, NLP, EMDR, Mindfulness and Coaching, Monica has successfully helped many people overcome all kinds of emotional, physical and physiological conditions, thus enabling her clients to unlock the full potential of their minds - enabling them to achieve Mind, Body and Soul Balance - so they can take control of their life and become the person they've dreamed of being.

Monica is associated with the National Eczema Society helping people take control of both the physical and psychological effects of skin conditions.

Over the years Monica has successfully used the Techniques in this book with her clients, and decided to put them together so she could share them with you.

Monica practices in London, and also consults over Skype/ FaceTime.

She is a Member of the BATTH GHR, GHSC, CNHC & The Royal Society of Medicine

Monica's contact details are:

Website:	www.hampsteadhypnotherapy.com
Facebook:	www.facebook.com/hampsteadhypno
Twitter:	@hampsteadhypno
LinkedIn:	Monica Black
Instagram:	Monicablack

Preface

The inspiration for My Little Book of Helpfulness came in the middle of a dark winter's night in January, 2016, around 3am and it can be attributed to two factors.

The first was - earlier in the day I had posted on North West London Network and Recommendations website the "Get that Feel Good Factor" **HELPFULNESS TECHNIQUE**. I received wonderful feedback from people especially one in particular from an amazing lady called Gail Hugman of Lessons Alive.

The second factor was, I was nursing a terrible cold — coughing, spluttering and unable to breathe, hence unable to sleep - when I had what could be called a 'light bulb' moment when Gail's comment hit me - I thought *"Over the years I've built up and used these exercises with my clients. They are structured in a simple to understand format, so why not put them all together into a little book, so I can share them with you"*

And so My Little Book of Helpfulness was born.

I hope, not only do you enjoy it, but that it helps you through your day-to-day life.

Thank you

Monica

Contents

3-Step Confidence Booster

This **HELPFULNESS TECHNIQUE** can be used to boost confidence very quickly using 'anchors'.

Anchors are very powerful. They bring back memories. A good example of an anchor is, maybe you suddenly hear some music or a song that you haven't heard for say 20 years. What happens? - you are suddenly 'transported' back to that moment when you first heard it, you relive that wonderful moment. Maybe a smell brings back a sweet memory. For me the smell is of cut grass – it reminds me of my childhood, or my grandmother's perfume – Chanel No. 5 and I'm immediately transported back to being a little girl playing in her bedroom.

We have all done or achieved things in our lives which, when we think back to them, gives us that **'wow'** or **'whoosh'** feeling. So what you can do is think of 3 separate instances when this had happened to you. Any experience that makes you feel good about yourself when you think of it and if you write this experience down, it will become even stronger and more real than when it is a thought. So

1. Write each experience down on an A4 sheet of paper. Place each sheet in a line on the floor. (it doesn't matter which order they are in).

2. Then stand behind the first sheet of paper looking down at your "feeling".

3. Relax and close your eyes.

4. Take yourself back to that experience. Be back in the experience. See what you saw, hear what you heard, feel what you felt. Maybe you can remember what you were wearing, what the weather was like, what time it was etc.

5. When you've got all the pertinent details about the experience let that ***"whoosh"*** feeling get bigger and stronger. Then when it's as big and as strong as you can make it press your thumb and index finger together on both hands (anchor). Hold for about 15 seconds.

6. Repeat the exercise for the remaining 2 experiences.

7. When you've gone through all 3 experiences, sit down, breath comfortably. Press your index finger and thumb together on both hands.

8. You should feel those good feelings every time you use that anchor.

You can do this whenever you feel you need a confidence boost.

MY NOTES

5-Minute Quick Phobia Cure

You can use this **HELPFULNESS TECHNIQUE** should you have a little phobia or are fearful of something.

1. Imagine you are sitting in the cinema, and you are going to see a movie.

2. This movie is about your phobia/fear and the movie just happens to be in black and white.

3. It has a beginning, middle and end.

4. The beginning is just before you experienced the incident and you are feeling safe and secure.

5. The middle is the incident itself.

6. The end is when the incident is over and you feel safe and secure again.

7. Now you understand what you need to do, you can start watching the movie from the beginning to the end.

8. Once its finished and you can see your still image at the end of the movie, float out of yourself to the projection booth and watch

the movie again, but this time, because you are in the projection booth, you are watching yourself sitting in the cinema watching yourself on the screen.

9. Watch the movie again from beginning to end. Observe how you feel, but because you are removed from the incident, you can actually watch the movie without a negative response. Again stop the movie at the end so that it is a still image.

10. Float from the projection booth, back into the screen and step into your still image which is positioned at the at the end of the movie.

11. Turn the movie into bright bold colours and run it rapidly backwards, (it should take no more than 5 seconds).

12. Repeat Step 11 several times.

13. When you've finished, test yourself by thinking of the event, incident, or memory that you were fearful of, and notice if your fear/phobia has lessened or gone.

14. You can repeat this exercise until you feel better.

MY NOTES

Banishing a Limiting Behaviour

This **HELPFULNESS TECHNIQUE** is useful when you feel you are identifying yourself with a Limiting Behaviour or emotion - say in the form of feeling your self-esteem has plummeted or maybe you have a behaviour that's holding you back.

For example, let's say you are feeling "unhappy" and this "unhappiness" seems to have had a "grip" on you, so if someone said to you *"Jane tell me about you"* you might very well think *"I'm an unhappy person"*. This is where this **TECHNIQUE** can help

What you want to be able to do, is really dis-identify from this limiting behaviour and identify with your positive attributes.

From now on let's call your Limiting Behaviour **LB**

Mark out a cross an A4 sheet of paper – just as you see on the next page. This cross represents your torso and has 4 quadrants - Top Right Quadrant, Top Left Quadrant, Bottom Right Quadrant and Bottom Left Quadrant.

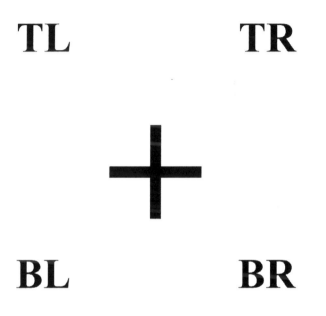

Your LB is usually felt in the centre of the cross. That is how you identify yourself. e.g. if someone came up to you and said *"Tell me about yourself"*, you would identify yourself with your LB. That little voice in your head could be saying *'Oh I have low self-esteem'* - however you are more than that Limiting Behaviour LB aren't you?

Now I know we hate to "*big ourselves up'* but for this exercise I want you to do just that:

1. Think of one positive attribute you have. Take your time. How does that make you feel when you think of that attribute? It can be absolutely anything that makes you feel good. Now, where would you like to feel and place that feeling- TR, TL, BR, BL.

2. Close your eyes and feel that feeling in the quadrant you have chosen. Really feel the feeling. Feel it getting bigger and stronger until it is completely filling up that quadrant. Hold it there.

3. Now, I can tell you that you are more than that one positive attribute. So what other attribute do you have that makes you feel good?

4. Think and choose that other positive attribute.

5. Repeat the exercise in the remaining 3 quadrants.

6. Feel the other positive attribute in your chosen quadrant and feel it getting bigger and stronger until it is completely filling up that second space.

7. Now feel the two attributes in both quadrants together.

8. Repeat Step 6, and repeat the exercise in the two remaining quadrants.

9. Feel all four positive attributes. Feel them getting bigger and bigger and stronger and stronger.

10. When all 4 quadrants are full with your positive feelings, test to see where your LB is. Has it lessened or gone and now you only feel those positive feelings?

11. If you can still feel something negative repeat the exercise until all your negativity has disappeared.

It's okay if you find you may need to do this a few times.

MY NOTES

Get that Feel Good Factor

Do you sometimes feel as if you are walking up hill wearing shoes made of cement? Or maybe you feel anxious, miserable, lacking in confidence and self-esteem, downtrodden, unhappy, sad, self-conscious or any other negative emotions?

Here is a quick and simple **HELPFULNESS TECHNIQUE** you can do to give yourself a boost.

1. Stand up.

2. Put your shoulders back.

3. Stand tall and feel as though a piece of string is pulling your spine and head up.

4. Pull your tummy in.

5. Close your eyes.

6. Breathe from your tummy (diaphragm) regularly, evenly and slowly.

7. See standing in front of you, the you, you want to be. The happy confident, secure etc. you.

8.   Now see, feel and sense that YOU.

9.   Take your time.

10. When you are ready walk into THAT YOU.

11. Feel and sense all those positive good feelings of that other you.

12. Once you do, press your thumb and index finger together and feel those good positive feelings getting bigger and stronger.

13. As you breathe slowly in, breathe in positivity and "lightness" and breathe out any "stuckness", "toxicity", anything that's not doing you any good.

14. Your breath is the anchor of your attention.

15. When you are ready, open your eyes and bring back with you the new you.

16. You can do this exercise as often as you wish.

MY NOTES

Help for Anxiety

This **HELPFULNESS TECHNIQUE** is to "re-calibrate" you when you feel as though you've lost control of what's happening to you at that moment.

LOOK AROUND YOU AND FIND:

1. 5 Things you can See
2. 4 Things you can Touch
3. 3 Things you can Hear
4. 2 Things you can Smell
5. 1 Thing you can Taste

MY NOTES

Inside Out

You can use this fun **HELPFULNESS TECHNIQUE** when you are feeling anxious, agitated, angry or even miserable and sad.

This is a short description as to how this exercise works.

Take our very ancient brain – well the prime purpose of all living things is to survive and procreate - our brain knows that we are in alignment – which means it knows that everything that is supposed to be on the left is on the left and everything that's on the right is on the right, this makes us in the perfect position to escape any predator that's after us and hopefully we survive!!

1. Sit in a comfy chair.

2. Cross your ankles.

3. Put your arms out in front of you with your palms facing each other.

4. With your arms still outstretched, cross them over at your wrists so the backs of your hands are facing each other.

5. Now turn your hands so your palms are facing and you can interlock your fingers.

6. Bend your elbows so your hands should now be under your chin.

7. Rest your head on the back of the chair.

8. Place your tongue on the roof of your mouth but touching your soft back palate.

9. Move your eyes in an arc from left to right whilst humming a tune – say Happy Birthday or just any old tune.

Yes I know you may feel silly and want to laugh – so laugh – it's okay to laugh and if you don't laugh that's okay too.

After about 3 minutes stop and see how you feel.

That negative feeling should have subsided or even gone.

MY NOTES

Instant Motivator

This **HELPFULNESS TECHNIQUE** teaches you how to motivate yourself whenever you need to.

Perhaps the greatest difficulty we all have is not being able to motivate ourselves, especially if the task in hand is difficult or boring.

1. Think of a task that you need to get done but you are making excuses not to do so because it feels pointless or tedious!! Maybe it could be something like tidying up your wardrobe or desk or even going to the gym.

2. Now take a moment and imagine you've completed the task.

3. How do you feel?

4. I'm sure you feel great because you've completed the task.

5. Emphasise that good feeling you are feeling because you've completed that tedious task. Make that feeling bigger and stronger making sure you see the task actually completed with you in the picture.

6. Now how do you feel about doing the task? You should feel all 'pumped up' and raring to go.

A good motivational tip is **never ever** use the word *'try'*. Try is one of the most negative words in our language. It's an instant de-motivator and sets us up to fail.

Instead use words such as "I can", "I will", "I am" and notice the difference to how you feel when you use them.

MY NOTES

Kick Out Intimidation 1

As so often happens in life, when we find ourselves facing an intimidating situation, an event or even more probably another person such as a bossy colleague, an overbearing 'aunt' or maybe someone in authority you can use this **HELPFULNESS TECHNIQUE.**

1. When this happens, the situation, event, person appears far bigger/taller, brighter/vibrant than it/they really are.

2. Now visualise that situation/event/person in front of you and as you look at them begin to shrink them down. Go on, shrink them down, down, down, down to the size of a little blue smurf with a squeaky little voice.

3. As you look at the smurf you see that it doesn't have any legs but it is balanced on a small roller ball.

4. Place it in a circle on the floor and see yourself walking around the smurf. You are tiptoeing around it but just the gentle vibration of your gentle footsteps causes the smurf to fall down.

Now how do you feel about that situation, event, person?

Keep doing the exercise until you do not feel fearful any more.

MY NOTES

Kick Out Intimidation 2

Another **Kick Out Intimidation HELPFULNESS TECHNIQUE** you can use would be:

1. See the situation/event/person that is making you fearful standing in-front of you, now;

2. Think of something funny that makes you laugh. It could be a song, a film, TV programme, anything at all.

3. Enhance that feeling that makes you happy - you can chuckle or even better laugh out loud.

4. Now think of the situation/event/person that was intimidating.

5. How do you feel now?

Laughter and/or amusement is a wonderful leveller and takes the "sting" out of uncomfortable situations.

MY NOTES

The Swish

This little **HELPFULNESS TECHNIQUE** gives you the ability to reprogramme negative thoughts, feelings and behaviours that aren't doing you any good, and which you feel you are now identifying with.

To start this exercise see your cue picture, sound or sensation.

Your Cue Picture is what triggers your issue – so you actually need to picture yourself with your unwanted behaviour. Now holding onto that behaviour:

- Close your eyes, and notice what you see, hear, feel when you see that picture.

- Get rid of it.

- Now see in front of you an image of how you want to be.

This image should be of all the behaviours, qualities and attributes that you believe you need to have so you can engage and sustain your desired outcome. In other words **see yourself doing the desired behaviour.**

- See that image on a screen in front of you.

- Then get rid of it.

Now for **THE SWISH HELPFULNESS TECHNIQUE**

1. Close your eyes.

2. Imagine a screen in front of you and on it is a picture of you doing your unwanted behaviour.

3. Put a picture of your new desired behaviour over it.

4. Make this picture **BIGGER** and **BOLDER**.

5. Very quickly pull down your desired behaviour with your right hand (if you are left-handed use your left hand) and shrink it down to the size of a postage stamp, which you are holding in your hand.

6. Throw your new desired behaviour, forcefully back over the image of your unwanted behaviour and as you do so, say very loudly "SWISH".

Repeat this at least 6 times very quickly, repeating "SWISH" every time you throw your desired behaviour over your unwanted behaviour.

NOW DO A REALITY CHECK – what image can you see on the screen? If you can see any part of the old unwanted behaviour keep doing the exercise until all you can see is your new desired behaviour.

SEE YOURSELF IN THE FUTURE – imagine yourself in the situation that gave you the unwanted behaviour. Ask yourself "how do I feel?" If there is any doubt, continue doing the SWISH until you feel fine.

Go on try it next time you're feeling "*uncomfortable*" and notice how much better you feel after this quick exercise.

MY NOTES

HELPFULNESS TECHNIQUES **to relax**

"Stop the World I Want to get Off"

You should do at least one of the following **RELAXATION HELPFULNESS TECHNIQUES** on a daily basis.

To get into the habit of doing this and what worked for me, was to make an appointment with myself in my diary at a time when I knew I'd got 5 - 15 minutes spare in my day, every day.

By doing this, I knew I'd succeed in being able to do at least one exercise because I'd made the 'appointment' at a time that was do-able, realistic and achievable for me.

MY NOTES

A Short Mindful Breathing Exercise

This is a Mindful Exercise which enables you to come back to your 'now' – to your present - by bringing your attention to your breath. When we breathe properly (from our diaphragm) our Stress levels go down and we become more focused, calmer and back 'in control'. This little exercise should take about 4 minutes.

Find somewhere comfortable to sit or lie down.

Close your eyes and take a couple of comforting breaths.

When you're ready, become aware of your body on the surface you are on.

Become aware of your back against the surface that your back is resting against.

Become aware of the back of your legs against the surface your legs are on.

If you are sitting, become aware of your feet on the floor.

If you are lying down become aware of the back of your heels resting on the surface they are resting on.

Become aware of your clothes on your body.

Maybe you can feel the air on your face and hands.

Become aware of all of these things

Now become aware of your breath coming and going, coming and going.

Maybe you can use as a focal point your nostrils because that's where the air enters your body.

Feel the air as it passes through up your nose and down to the back of your throat and continues to your lungs and tummy.

You have nothing to do, nothing to prove, nothing to fear.

You are just taking some time out to take some time in and being aware of your breath.

Your breath is the anchor of your attention.

When you feel you are ready, bring your attention fully back to your surroundings and carry on with your day.

MY NOTES

"Just Be"

Lie down so your feet are slightly raised above your head. You can put them on some pillows for example. Turn off your phone and get rid of pets, partners and any nuisances that may be around and could disturb you.

Remember.......

THIS IS YOUR TIME

If you're the sort of person who gets "ants in your pants" and can't relax after 5 minutes - then do it for 5 minutes. If you can do it for longer then that's great.

If you want to play some soft soothing music that's fine too so go ahead.

And put on the music.

Don't fall asleep.

JUST BE

You'll be amazed how much better you feel.

But remember if you can't relax then don't force it - because it will only make you more stressed and that's defeating the purpose.

The reason your feet are raised, is because it helps the circulation to get going, thereby bringing more oxygen to all parts of your body. It also helps the lymphatic system - which gets rid of toxins, to get going too, so aches and pains are eased.

REMEMBER

Slow down and breathe slowly and from your stomach

MY NOTES

The Balloon

(Don't do this exercise if you are frightened of Balloons.)

This easy and most effective technique is based on the simple notion of proper breathing. If your breathing is slow and controlled, you will begin to feel relaxed.

When we breathe in, our lungs inflate and when we breathe out they deflate. Well this exercise is based on that movement.

Sit down and close your eyes.

Place your right hand on your tummy and your left hand on your chest.

Imagine a balloon that just happens to be your favourite colour in front of you.

Breathe slowly and deeply using the following technique:

As you breathe in through your nostrils imagine a balloon inflating in front of you.

As you breathe out see that balloon deflating.

On your third out breath, breathe out any stress, anxiety, negativity or 'stuckness' you feel as the balloon deflates.

Do this for a minute or two – you'll be surprised at how relaxed you feel afterwards.

MY NOTES

Countdown

This **HELPFULNESS TECHNIQUE** only takes a couple of minutes to do. It is really helpful when you are experiencing Anxiety or Stress and it can also help you fall back to sleep if you wake up in the middle of the night.

Make sure you are comfortable.

Focus your attention effortlessly on a spot opposite you, just a little bit above eye level.

Take 3 slow deep breaths. As you exhale on your third breath let your eyes close.

Now see in your mind's eye a piece of paper or a screen or a black/white board, and on it are the numbers 25 down to 1. On your out breath tick each number off starting with 25, and you'll find with each tick you'll become more and more relaxed.

When you reach 1, just sit quietly for a few minutes, then once you feel ready, in your own time open your eyes. You should now feel peaceful, calm and refreshed.

MY NOTES

Wise Person

On a final note, you should know you have a **Wise Person** inside of you and your **Wise Person** will never, ever fail you.

So when in doubt about anything at all:

- find somewhere quiet to sit;

- close your eyes;

- breathe slowly;

- relax;

- with every out breath allow yourself to become more settled;

- allow your **Wise Person** to come to the fore;

- your **Wise Person**, will tell you what to do.

Listen to what he/she has to say, he/she will always guide you onto your right path so you will know how to move forward.